Concurring Beasts

THE LAMONT POETRY SELECTION FOR 1971
OF THE ACADEMY OF AMERICAN POETS

This distinguished award, sponsored "for the discovery
and encouragement of new poetic genius," is made every
year to an American poet who has not yet had a book of
poetry published. The judges for 1971 were Michael
Benedikt, Richard Howard and James Merrill.

Concurring Beasts

Poems by Stephen Dobyns

New York *1972* Atheneum

Acknowledgements are due to the following publications in whose pages some of the poems previously appeared:

CAFE SOLO: *The Conviviality of Cows.*
THE CHICAGO REVIEW: *After the War with the Eskimos; Explaining the Nature of Evidence* (under the title of *Straight But Not Blue*).
THE ENGLISH RECORD: *To Close My Hand.*
THE IOWA REVIEW: *Litany.*
KAYAK: *The Annunciation; Connections; Hotel; Leaving the Bar and Low Life at Closing, I Unsuccessfully Pursue Sainthood; Refusing the Necessary; Talking Around You; Travelling Light with the Good Saint, A Seasonal Tribute.*
THE LITTLE MAGAZINE: *The Indispensables.*
MINNESOTA REVIEW: *The Crossing; Weather Watch.*
NORTH AMERICAN REVIEW: *Aid and Assistance in Difficult Times; Forming An Entrance/Epiphany; The Way It Goes or The Proper Use of Leisure Time.*
NORTHEAST: *Beginnings and Ends of Departure.*
POETRY: *Contingencies; Counterparts; Finding the Direction; Name-Burning; Passing the Word; Taking a Crack at It; Waking, the Cheering Begins; When You're Dancing Make the Whole World Dance with You; The Ways of Keys.*
POETRY NORTHWEST: *Continue By Waking; In the Hospital; In the Morning; Late Planting; Making An End; Of Stones.*
TRACE: *High Society, Iowa City, Iowa.*

for E. & J.

Contents

PART THREE

PART FOUR

PART FIVE

Part One

*"Does not all art come when a nature . . .
exhausts personal emotion in action
or desire so completely that something
impersonal, something that has nothing to
do with action or desire, suddenly
starts into its place, something which is
as unforeseen, as completely organized,
even as unique, as the images that pass
before the mind between sleeping and
waking."*—Yeats

*"Experience, already reduced to a group
of impressions, is ringed round for each
one of us by that thick wall of personality
through which no real voice has ever
pierced on its way to us, or from us
to that which we can only conjecture to be
without. Every one of these impressions is
the impression of the individual in his
isolation, each mind keeping as a solitary
prisoner its own dream of a world."*
—Pater

*"I do not ask of God that he should
change anything in events themselves, but
that he should change me in regard to things,
so that I might have the power to create
my own universe, to govern my dreams,
instead of enduring them."*—Nerval

Forming An Entrance/Epiphany

Push him through. The eye of the needle's before us,
opening onto Nebraska, billiard tables, grain elevators
rising above the holy. His arm first, then shoulder—
yesterday's dinner on a brown plate. Do not listen
to his noises of comfortable apartments, necessary warmth.
We can do without him. Now his head and other arm.
His eyes are aware of it: the back of the unwaking beast
murmuring to itself. He will walk on it with grass feet,
thinking of cities and small rooms. The earth will
grow to him. Now his waist, hips. We have promised him
a new place, waiting for him—people after midnight
in lighted houses. Now his legs, feet. We watch him
fall off into the dirt roads, a nest of machinery
turning towards him, embracing him. He will be happy,
renew us with his discoveries and far places. He
will remain in our mirrors, still connected, mixing
our voices over the long wires, catching their echoes.
The fields gather to us, opening, forming an entrance.

Beginning

There are wedding rings brighter
than the eyes of that blue-eyed baby.
His feet are on the ceiling. Dangle
to your Papa. We shall shut the door
on you one last time. Do you give in?
Outside, our lawn is a bed of nails
each pryed from a succession
of past houses. Remember how they fell?
Shouted down, pushed, whenever there
was nothing else to do. Harsh words.
Our grass is rusty with worry. Show baby
the mower along with his first steps.
Our own distances will measure them.
Is he out of his closet? Is he
blossoming? He needs time to grow
to our errors. We shall teach him
and let him get used to our ways
before taking his toys and small flowers:
stars deep in his darkening hands.

Leaving the Bar and Low Life at Closing, I Unsuccessfully Pursue Sainthood

Keep your laughter to yourself, Dixieland Band.
Uncle Charlie on the tuba has no time to wave
goodbye as, taking my change, I leave you
to your Umpas and amoral keys. This is my last
singalong. Sister Immaculata has passed the window
and I must follow on this stormy night where sirens
complain of nebulous somewheres. Yggdrasil,
the holy tree, still stands. The squirrel still carries
insults from eagle to serpent and back. Sister,
there's time for one last blast before the horn.
Slow your steps so I may reach you. We shall be
transformed and lunge toward sainthood like fish against
a southern beach. Odin didn't lose that eye for nothing.
The skirts of your dark habit turn a final corner.
Rejection's cheap when the town's shut down. Already,
the last taxis and cleaning women have run off
to their grey and nefarious garage. Rattle
those bones, Darkness, and eat another star for me.
I'm whistling Dixie among yesterday's litter.
Sister, where are your smiles and promises now?
Half the morning has been answered. No book or mother
ever told me there were streets like these.

The Annunciation

Without walls, his office is marked by red lines
on the floor. Everything above me grows darker.
I've come to have a tooth fixed. He calls
himself a dentist. His face rises over me,
glasses with black frames, a pipe. His clothing
is black. He asks about my tooth, the quality
of peace. I speak of the change in my leg,
show it to him. The leg is serpentine, covered
with feathers. Red arrows point to its heart. His assistant
crouches, sitting on his haunches, a mongoloid face,
hundreds of smiles travel his mouth. They
leave the room. I get up, go to the mirror, a smaller
mirror in my hand, open my mouth, look inside.
People wave from the tops of white buildings,
pink lawns stretch into valleys. There is no city so lovely.
Far to the west an Aztec temple, the House of the Dwarf,
more beautiful than symmetry. I wander through its gardens,
white tiers rising above me. The walls are rough
with frescoes, old processions, celebrations in low relief.
It is all falling down. The priests are chanting,
the sound echoes through its tunnels. They cover the altars.
I leave it, return the mirror. The chair talks
of its blood. I walk to it, climb up, its pneumatic
contours touch, form themselves around me. My head
falls back; the great light erases the room. The doctor
has not returned. We are waiting, we are all waiting.

In the Hospital

He has refused absolution and moved piece by piece
into silence. His tongue lies motionless, disconnected;
there was nothing left to say. Unable to leave each other,
his hands nestle together, small animals, a joint urgency.
He will not stand or walk, there is no reason for it.
He has retired into himself, discovered the horizons
of corners and dark rooms. When they take him out,
the walls go with him, keeping their tight enclosure.
No food will tempt him. The nurses are white birds
he no longer thinks of touching. Sometimes he is
spoken to. It will rain. He can hear the thunder,
see clouds brighten and fall back. He shuts down
his fields, his dark barns. The thunder passes, leaves him
to his planting. He is aware of the sun, can feel
its benediction. There a tree, there a river, there a tree.

Contingencies

on LES ENERVÉS DE JUMIÈGES
by Évariste Vital Luminais

There is a picture, a French painting, showing
two men on a raft over a river of light brown,
which is not mud but the absence of color
within color; beneath a sky drained of its blue—
water drained from a pond, blood from the body;
and the river moves between fields
which have been cut; trees aware of their dying
and no longer quarreling with it. The two men
lean back in the positions they find themselves,
and in their eyes it doesn't matter, in their legs
it doesn't matter. They have been hamstrung,
the old punishment. Their only knowledge
is the knowledge of water: the river moving
to the sea and the sea moving to accept their punishment,
now insignificant. Death has ceased to be an issue.
There is no knowledge of crime. There is only
the bare fact of landscape, the fatal lack
of possibility, and the end which is water.
Death is a small door opening through their eyes.

Sometimes, moving between two places—to class,
the store, to some person who seems to possess
the knowledge and cunning of light; and noticing
leaves drained and past color, the grey of concrete;
I think of this painting. And as I raise my foot
for the next step there is a slight trembling,
as if the Earth were resettling on its Nordic tree
or if the tree itself were twisting away
from the creatures that gnaw it. Suddenly,
I step into a world where everything is fragile,

leans toward breakage. There are long cracks
stretching before me, paths of crystal leading
to or from the dark elms, the quiet of the sea.
For a short while my hands grow empty and nothing
will fit them, no stone or other hand. I become
a glass target among all things pointed and haphazard.

Travelling Light with the Good Saint,
A Seasonal Tribute

There are bells now, and a few words for St. Jude,
patron of lost causes. Ring them like women
with a welcoming hand. Doors open like buds,
it being spring, the blossoming season. Hello, weather.
All doors are asexual in winter. Across new fields, visitors
are streaming. They could be flags for all their waving.
Let us sit down in a warm place and expand
upon ourselves. Let us feed, grow like crocuses
on kind words. Let us build a small church of sticks
and a clay image of the saint. Give him a candle
and a big cigar. He knows the right people
like we are, will be. My bag is packed.
Loki, the trickster, is in chains. Goodbye, Coyote,
your paw's in a trap, a temporary measure.
But you won't catch the last train, that train,
and I'm waving from the engine with my itinerary
of unspellable places. The mud saint sits
on a box beside me, flinging smiles to the weather.
His feet don't reach the floor. We are
leaving. My hand's on the throttle. My head's
out the window. Ring all bells. Welcome stones. We're
heading toward summer like it's the last one.

Making An End

Furless, skin the color of fresh cream, the horses
have not yet begun to decompose. Three men
stand near them, jab them with sticks. Spiders
in white face mount the horses and three men,
laughing into paper hats. Crows eat everything
in sight. Watch your feet. I hunt children
with a bow and arrow, looking for what I've
already forgotten. Sometimes I see their faces
in the trees—drooping moustaches, tattoos, Rosa,
1941. After a rain the trees turn to neon, green
breaking from their leaves like loyalty, Madagascar.
Death is a young man in a red shirt, a seller of tickets.
He smiles from his library, proud of his Dickens
and Gautier, delaying a greeting until later.
Three children follow me, dragging a cart, carrying
one of the horses; red and yellow streamers
cover the wheels, pieces of television antennas.
A firemen's band plays "Sweet Abilene." The crows
begin on the ground. I join the crowd in front of
the coroner's, also a young man. He passes comic hats
to lines stretching back to the cities, legends
of cement. Having devoured its rays, the crows
begin on the sun itself. A festival of waiting.
Colored lanterns float over our heads; painted faces
becoming the faces of the crowd. The coroner touches
a switch. Someone blinks off, then another and
another. Wild anticipation.

Continuing Anyway

He has become himself in clothes. He
has memorized city directories and may
take on the qualities of houses.
He is partial to brick which is
the texture of his suit. Walk with him.
He has become what he is dressed for:
a gathering of formalities, a worship
of breathing. Each day he avoids the papers
which he must do if he is to continue.
He has rejected the concept of Japan
and similar subjects. Discovered suddenly
in his breast pocket, he decides to join himself.
He watches you from his tie—
green and smelling of Kansas.
His laughter reaches equally far. His days
are dressed in your inaccuracies. At night,
when you have reached your uncertain beds,
he rests in his closet, hanging, smiling;
thankful of tweed and mothballs;
unbreakably lined with silken definitions.

Talking Around You

All the lines are down between here and Dawson, skins
of snakes, bicycle tracks. There has been a reckoning.
You are no longer there for me to hear. Listen,
we shall mend them. I dust off my intentions,
apply polish. They gleam like small silver tongs.
They are my best. You must tell me about them
when there is time. Your mouth moves, forming words.
We must replace the wires, tie them to strong people.
Take these from my hands, my little tongs. I said
take these from my hands. You turn away. Take them
to those others standing outside us, telephone poles,
fence posts. I can't quite hear what they are saying.
The wires are down. There are no strong men to guide us.
Let me look into your face, your eyes. You must
accept my promises, these small gifts neatly plated.
We will use your hair, spin it, link the threads
to our separate buildings, open the doors. No one
will know of it. Listen. You don't understand.
Your hand then. This is my house, touch it. Notice
the locks and iron hinges. These doors open
only for you. Notice the chairs, their easy comfort.
You don't understand. We must wait for the right time.
Someone will come. Already I see dust on the ridge,
it may be the first. I have your future carefully planned.
There are warm areas and welcomings. We will be patient,
keep to ourselves. Somewhere, even now, people
are thinking of us. It's only a matter of time.

Part Two

". . . *the mind cannot stop short of an extreme, because it has to deal with an extreme, with a conflict of forces left to themselves, and obeying no other but their own inner laws. . . .*"

Taken out of context from
Carl von Clausewitz's ON WAR

Waking, the Cheering Begins

Suddenly, rising, another rises with him,
out of his chair, the room, a bullet in its chamber,
waiting to go off.
        He can feel doors opened,
feel his other preparing himself, the smell
of oil, strips of cloth.
        Of the tunnels before him
all but one will be destroyed. He must
choose between them, has forced himself
to the decision, but sees no difference
between them.
        In the next room a faucet
repeats the meaning of silence, not
forgetting it, repeating it again.
        Walls
are breaking up within him, spaces opened,
distances he had never dreamed of.
        A fair ground,
a circle of striped tents, ferris wheels;
a man selling song-birds, each with a leg
tied to the ground.
        He rides in an open car,
surrounded by crowds, standing motionless,
holding flags, signs; making no noise, their
faces familiar.
        He tries to spell out the signs—
the air is a hand about to enclose him—spell
out the signs, ending the silence.
        The sun falls
like a target, dying the faces red. Someone
is moving through the crowd. A slight wind
rustles the flags. The crowd waits for the signal,

for the cheering to begin.

He sees his other
near him, turns towards him, begins to move
towards him, crosses his sights.

Connections

Two days of listening to a police radio
and everyone around me is a killer. I have
walked this far, I must go slower. People
hang onto bodies that won't be with them
long. Their own and all the others.
Give me your hand. I hold it like liquid
with the same result. My own hand drips
like water from a tree after a short rain.
Green becomes the color of decay. The forest
surrounds us. Standing on the fire tower
in the state park, I see a doe moving
beneath me. All twigs are pointed at it.
The ground can swallow it. If I shout
its sky will crumble. I refuse to breathe.
Nearby, hunters with bows and arrows rehearse
their comic lines: Who will grace our fenders?
Who will hang upside down in our immaculate
front yards? Their arrows have captured
the wind and its music. Their faces are like
drums, or clocks ticking. Their faces drip;
the noise of static on a radio. If I shout
my own sky will splinter. Silence? I fill
my lungs like a swimmer diving to the bottom.

Forming an Entrance/Epiphany

There is no sky today. Echoes of birds
worry their way northward. They must have
everything repeated many times. You are here
and elsewhere, your face breeding like fear.
It is not for nothing that I keep my hands
raised for the fall. This is a country of smaller wars.

You have your office and ranch house, your foreign car
and family. You are still not necessary. I see
your face in a photograph from the war, surrounded
by soldiers convinced by their smiles. Later
there will be that look of faint surprise
as you meet the world and lie down to be counted.

The colors of blood are legion. Of necessity
your name must be also. Choose any direction
and it will lead to the heart. We call it a diamond.
Placed on the ground, we heap stones around it,
logs over it. What loss to a two car family?
We bring flowers. In error, people will call it a funeral.

Days pass, fires to be tended—their flames
like small fingers looking for your eyes. You have
already torn them from you. All things desire
to be surrounded by stone. There is rain on my hands.
There is the steady thud of birds falling into hills
sloping with sheep. We memorize the art of decay.

A swift and pervading grey slips through my fingers,
cloud covered and accustomed to war. A bone
is my weapon. It may not have been mine. Each end
is sharpened and carefully aimed. The ground
and pine bows hiss a warning. There are rumours
of summer. There are seasons no longer acceptable.

Taking a Crack at it

We have discovered dark paint for the sky.
Rats hide in sewers, refusing what we
leave them. In Washington, a man breaks up
Monday, Tuesday, Wednesday. He is smaller
than necessary. People keep writing about it,
pouring their words into the streets. It rises
above our ankles. On the corner, a man remembers
flowers, and hurries home to tell others who won't
be his friends for long. Make the walls ready.
Board over the windows. Even if open
the sun would reject them. If I walk all day
looking for clean water, I will find people
throwing themselves into it. Stones are safer.
They sink to the bottom. We have shut ourselves
into our eyes and shut our eyes after us.
Nobody's watching. We have grown so ignorant
that we can't build a gibbet. Hangman's rope
comes cheap. Eyes locked, we rock ourselves
in a cat's cradle of compromise and silence.

High Society, Iowa City, Iowa

Peter Cooley lives on Dodge Street south,
with his wife, Jacqueline, and small daughter.
Although a walkable distance away, I drive.
My white VW bus rolls down the street,
an intractable tank, impervious to degrees. Snipers
see me coming, shoot, run for cover. The twin guns
over my head-lights shatter their black frocks.
Diplomas batter my windows and doors, converge
on my tires. I accelerate to thirty-five, ignore
the light, turn to the children with small knives,
sharp teeth, spray their faces through the trees. Coming
to a stop, a small conflict with a Doberman Pinscher
and a ten-foot whip. I run up the steps, knock, Peter answers.
Bursting through the room, I see Nicole, the daughter,
rising. My mind is as one that dances. Machetes
drop from her hands like wild petals.

After the War with the Eskimos

Having forced the peace, the Eskimos
are riding down to greet us, mounted
on great bears, gentle as clocks, legs
like the legs of the statue of liberty.
We will speak to them of seals, wallowing
in fish-tanks, and convince them we are
pro-seal, pro-igloo, and will, in time
be pro-Eskimo.

                We see the first
high above us. His face like a nugget
taken from the hands of a drunken miner.
pitted, benevolent; then the others,
as warm as dollars waiting for our words.
Come to our houses, meet our daughters.
Let your bears make sport with our dogs,
our cousins half removed.

The Conviviality of Cows

In the ungreased field they cling
to the grass to keep from falling,
so many shoes in a green box.
They graze, anxiously planning, touching
their backs in close conversation.
Two go over the hill, another follows.
In the high tower of guns and great lights
a guard shoots a short burst
to keep them from the fence.
They turn back. The fence is lined
with pheasants. There are no miles here.
At night, if the trucks don't come,
back to the barn, banging horns,
kicking soft hooves for company.

Late Planting

Birds are weaving their wings
and sharp beaks through my shadows.
In the distance a tractor unwinds itself
into green fields, cows drift
ahead with a semblance of haste.
Now driving, I turn the wheel
of the tractor, proceed over the gates,
the roads, to the edges of town.
The streets erupt behind me,
people look up from their parcels
and white string. Lifting myself,
I step over the tractor, the telephone
poles, spread out over the town.
People retreat to dubious nests
and welcomes. Buildings scatter.
Falling into the trees, the sun
signals for help. All over
birds start singing in beautiful fury.

The Way It Goes or
The Proper Use of Leisure Time

Now all my words are bricks
and I have built myself a small penitentiary.
I still refuse to be penitent but
take pleasure in diddling the idea.

If my cat continues to become human,
I will kill it and rid myself
of its echoes. The cat
understands this and will become more human.

Instead of barred windows, there are mirrors;
instead of reflections, there are doubts.
They wear belted and double-breasted raincoats,
sharp hats drawn over their eyes.

I have sent my cat on an errand of mercy,
a few coins and a note around his neck
to the Pope. My doubts tell me he is lounging
in a bar waiting for the King to die.

With an intense effort I turn the bricks
back into words. They flutter and fall
like dying bats. Here is one called
Help, and another, Haste.

I refuse to accept them or see them as mine.
This is a poem about being alone.

Extending the Coming Times

The three-toed Governor of Alabama eyes
the perjured hassock of our intent,
swaddled in old declarations. Mirrors
crowd his feet, gilt slippers lifted
to his nation's effort. The National
Rifle Association owes him a medal
for modesty and daring, shots beyond
the call of duty. All over the country
horses retire to dark caves and swamps,
huddle over the coals of poems.
They know of hounds and blond boys with sticks.
At Churchill Downs the last Derby Winner
finishes a last cigarette. The Governor
raises his sword.

The Indispensables

*"The Zapparoni Works manufactured robots
for every imaginable purpose."*
ERNST JUENGER, The Glass Bees.

These people stand softly,
moving together, speaking together,
as light reflected in the water at evening,
always at your command. They may be used
at parties as a crowd. They're popular.
They'll talk quietly to your guests.
Silence will not separate them.
This one may be used by itself.
Notice the hair, the easy motion
of the chin. It may have either sex.
You may trust him. He will keep
your secrets and is a person with whom
you could steal. Like part of you,
he will always be with you, may have
your face, pass for you at meetings,
or in the street when you cannot move freely.
These things are necessary to you.
Believe me, I am your friend. I will
sell you a life cheaply; an opening
down through the roots of your skin.

George Wallace Visits Lansing, Michigan

after Vaillant.

1

The face of the new capitol office building bends
to its vanishing point; a de Chirico painting, washed
of its color, surrounded by stone. Clerks glance narrowly
toward empty streets, then lower their blinds;
rifle-sized windows, thin cracks in the walls.

2

A girl in orange shorts wheels a crippled woman
between the wall and the void of the street. Their faces
are as fragile as glass; a single expression
would crack them. The only sound is the hum and rattle
of the collapsible chair. Each wheel reflects stone;
each spoke a needle gaining speed.

3

Three buses race between stone, their lights blazing
with the rage of awakened mastodons. The buses
are filled with white faces; each a scrap of paper
scribbled with fear, hope of retaliation. A shout
would tear them. Police cars surround them like flowers.

4

The police of Highland Park have made their pilgrimage:
ninety miles through land where each rock is a hand
stretched out in brotherly compulsion. We have
slept too long. Arriving with hair and pistols greased,
they bend and place two hundred dollars at his feet.

Litany

Wherever we go, we must go in darkness.
We have eaten our candles. Cattle must always
be accepted. They are useless and as benign
as Christmas. Rats are hated not for their faults,
which are ours, but because they are consistent
in our virtues. In the cellars of misers
each rat is a hero. I shall be such a hero
with a black wagon and bell, waking the streets
and accepting the living. We read of directions
in books. I know of roads that shut down at night,
go off on their own explorations.
They are modest and no super highways
are among them. Bite into an apple
and a small voice shouts hello. Be respectful
to your food. Run down the street shouting
and everyone shuts their doors. Join them
in darkness. On the roads we have taken,
cities are the last stages of the cattles' journey.
Chicago welcomes their conventions. The right roads
will discover my humility, tell me their secrets.
Eventually, when people reach Chicago after years
of darkness, cattle will drive wagons with streamers
and favors. Avoiding the occasion, I will go north
with a road in Wyoming. It will tell early stories.
Each step will brighten toward the sun.

Continue By Waking

Continue by waking. There are cracks in the sea wall;
fish appear before us full of elderly benevolence.

(Someone wants a quarter but he won't get it.)
Take the palms of my hands, the nails. Plant them.
A lemon tree of Spanish singing birds, a circus tent.
Nothing will grow but it's good to believe.

From the train window the telephone poles continue
their message; crooked poles, short poles. Just
as I begin to understand we reach the city.
A memory of horses; someone wanting to get out.

Take the soles of my feet, the callouses. Nail them
to your door. California poppies, butter running
over the ground, melons, a donation of feathers.
No one will come but you don't know that.

Continue by car. Small deaths swept up before us
by trucks carrying oranges, pig iron; not arteries
but seams, the seams of our country. Distances are
longer each year. New York is a negative concept.

Take my arms, legs, shred them, weave them into
a new coat, colorless, sturdy. You will not need it.
Flies breed in it. Chairs need hands. Doors ask
for matches. Insurance has never been so expensive.

In cities, buildings reveal themselves to birds,
pigeons, carrying bits of cement, fertilizing them,
letting them grow. On foggy nights they bury themselves
in cloud, talk quietly, question falling.

Take my head, body, scoop it out, fill it with dirt—
a window box. Then plant the eyes. All that I know
will grow before you. Trees of my skin. Fields
spell out my name. Flowers like yours. Sell them.

To Close My Hand

Dogs of large benevolence, spaniels and dark hounds,
bringing bones shining with goodness, small tokens
from the leash. Who am I to close my hand?

To you, with the pockets of your skin gleaming
in a dying sun; red birds searching for diamonds,
twilight—why should I ease my kindness?

Small yellow men return bits of metal we have
given them. We count out their bodies; the skins
of animals, beavers; the rising cost of hats. Who
am I to close my hand?

To myself I present the other hand. It meets, enters
like a courtesan, whispers a few public secrets,
then gives, then sleeps. Why should I close it?

Or you, a stranger, with your myth and stoney name,
what can you give me? A flag to sleep on, the quiet
of long fields, the touch of horses to close my hand.

Part Three

For many;
For Gérard's Adrienne and Saléma,
Jenny Colon the actress and the
Queen of Sheba

Your Place

Farther away than the table between us, you stand
on the slope, shading your eyes; mountains are your
natural habitat. Behind you, the rocks are hung
with your colors—dark browns and greys. You have
made this place, raised stones over known paths.
Its weather surrounds you, its mists, the chill
of its valleys. The dogs are friendly only to you.
Deep within the caves white flowers turn to your care,
bend quietly among each other. You must be careful
to keep them hidden even from yourself. Above you
great birds wind among peaks, brushing the tips
with dark wings. Their faces are more than bird-like,
predatory. Like secrets, they come unasked. You do not
control them, not even their flight within you,
those flower-eaters, dressed in your fears, the presence
of those caves, the light of which your darkness
is the counterpart.

In the Morning

You pick up your purse. I speak. You smile.
Your laughter breaks from my house like masses
of red birds, flocking over Iowa City. You
go after it, over the nested roofs, buildings
subject to urban renewal, buzz the power plant
chimney. Give it a shove. Scarlet feathers
filter through the air, brush passing heads.
People trod along, cars purr. You may touch them
if you wish. Kleenex catches in the wake
of your joy. I shout, "Look up!" Someone
walks down the center of a side-street, avoiding
the bricks that have been after him for years.
He hears me shout, stands transfixed. You fall
all over him.

Aid and Assistance in Difficult Times

Not just words but facial expressions—these
I will send to you upon need; carefully packed
in stone jars with drawings from the old masters—
Dachau, Dresden. The exhaustion of trees is telling,
but it is not my story. The elms have nearly
completed their protest. They stretch their branches,
but refuse the sun. Sparrows drop from them
like seeds. There are gifts for any occasion.
We have tamed our animals, drawn their claws
for our easier needs. Most dogs are sleeping.
We rarely eat what we kill. Mythological creatures
sink deeper and deeper into the mud of our learning.
Sympathy has no alphabet. Do not ask the obvious.
Wherever you go, you will be unlimited.
We must support each other in our errors.
I shall send aid and comfortable sayings
for the holiday seasons. Already there is snow
collecting in easy preparation. Two jars
with half smiles have been wrapped and labeled.
Not all the animals are missing. There
is a rope from the clouds. There is a griffin
carved upon the handle in my hand.

The Place Between Us

You sit as I do
but across the room.
Between us the silence
turns with the hunger
of great birds, their darkness
drops away at our feet.
Do not cry here.
There is too much space
for words, no bottom
for them to fall to.
We know the pit,
have carefully placed the stakes
with our own hands.

Explaining the Nature of Evidence

After the tables and chairs
voted to march on Pittsburgh,
the two rabbits grew a lawn
of their own and the barns waltzed
off through fields of ribald song.
All this happened yesterday,
and today I speak to you
about it. You sit, smiling,
roses growing from your head,
big black petals, grand pianos
with ebony keys. I sit,
talking quietly, my tongue
burning great holes in my mouth;
black birds drift through, batting at
the petals with heavy wings.
A grey Pomeranian
wanders in, bored and hungry,
looks once, then goes out again.
Your eyes soften. I speak of
the air pushing around us.
Somebody whistles, the black
roses turn in on themselves,
float off. I keep explaining.
You ask, what? You don't know who
I talk to, talking to you.

The Crossing

We hear it approaching and stop,
wrapped in the car around us.
As yet, only the eyes are visible,
one straight, the other revolving up
and across the tattered landscape:
dark backyards with their bicycles
and sprawling tires, machinery,
the grey ends of fields. A cat's eye,
dispassionate, disinterested. We sit
between two stations. The train
breaks over us, brushes light
over us and passes; the last car
disappearing near the woods. Slowly
our silence frees itself, moves forward.

Weather Watch

Between the two barns the air
is colder, a brighter color
on clear nights when the wind
hangs heavy with waiting.
It calls at a pitch
only dogs can hear. Time's
passing. They lie dreaming,
twitching their dark paws,
but cannot relay the message.
The air thickens. Our fields
are yellow with a brittle frost.
Soon there will be no words
to speak of.

Travelling

The lath is in thin short strips
and old, as the house is. Layers
of dust cover it like skin;
stones, pieces of cement. I
am on the dark side looking in.
You walk, trying the floor
with quick steps, the locked desk
and empty dresser, uncertainly,
like someone who has lost or
forgotten something important.
The house moves with you. It's
dark outside. Trees reach toward
the open window, almost
touching it, waving good-bye.

Refusing the Necessary

Becoming the river, we are the river.
Unable to accept it, we are drowning.
Your long hair floats on the surface—
sentences in a book I haven't read.
You ask for help. I can do nothing for you.
The river passes between high banks,
tree and fog bound. It passes over the tops
of intricate buildings. We can see the people,
but not their faces. They are shouting.
We can't make out their words. Fragments
of words float all around us. We are
those fragments. The language is foreign.
We have waited too long for our decisions.
We have waited too long after the last boats.
We are afraid to surface or seek the bottom.
Insubstantial, we are not enough to cling to.
Foghorns continue their warnings:
the house is burning, the king is sick.
Without daylight, we have forgotten the sun,
accepted a darker place. Between the surface
and bottom, we may hang forever.

Beginnings and Ends of Departure

*"Each individual is a composite
of many separate personalities."*

A knocking on the door, on the inside
of the door; a small fool's voice
wanting to get out. Again, they explain
impossibilities.

        (She is that lovely,
as lovely as light breaking upon water,
miles of it; a single ray, red, darting
quickly, then gone. They will not
question it.)

        So he continues, drum-like,
until the rest, unable to listen, begin
to leave, opening back windows, finding
paths through the cellar, too quietly
to be heard.

        At a place in the forest,
bears perform rituals of departure,
the voyage of winter; all in a circle,
each to a separate music. One joins them.

Another finds a city, drained of its color;
walks between the buildings, letting
his hand run over the stones, looking
for a permanent place among the stones.

Another in a garden, pulling at flowers,
staring into them, throwing them aside.
Each hits the ground—yellow poppies,

lavender—and closes, fist-like.
He will not stay long.

                    And others,
all turning to definite distractions—
tunneling to the hearts of mountains, old
military companies—choosing each place
as special; the binding but cut-rate freedom.

And still he continues: the steady knocking,
the small voice, rhythmatic, unable to stop,
continuing on the inside of the door. She is
that lovely.

Part Four

HOTEL

I

First coming they are always together, no sound
will separate them. They don't notice the walls
or marble columns. They move through the people,
not seeing them. The walls are red, covered
with pictures of small animals, statues
of animals surround them. In touching her
his hand is met by her skin, can't go farther.
People ask questions. There is no sound.
The silence presses around them, pushes itself
between them. He can still touch her hand,
let his own move up her arm. Their feet
are covered in the carpeting. A man comes
and tells them that everything has been
taken care of. The floor slopes in toward the wall,
red chairs rise above them. He can barely
hear what is being said.

II

Can someone tell me of the yellow room,
show me the stairs? There are great dogs
outside the door, black with golden collars.
The room is filled with velvet children,
faces borne by the wind.

————————————

I have seen the concierge in his place of keys,
scraps of letters cover his walls. All our names
are known to him. He has seen the corners
of our rooms. A gold key hangs from his neck
below white teeth. Doors belong to him.

————————————

Someone must know of the north attic
with its windows and stars. During the day
the light is called sun. You can hear
the rustling of spiders. They have a city
and control the movement of rooms.

————————————

I have been to the kitchens, seen the great stoves.
All day, oxen turn on the fires, kettles
boil the tears of children. A plate
of clear glass catches the steam,
cools it to a heavy yellow.

————————————

I have seen a room with a yellow light
revolving on a long chain. A room filled
with people leaping to catch its rays
in small bags. They talk of cellars,
corners too dark for life.

There is a place of catwalks and round
buildings. You never see the ground, but move
quickly into the buildings.
The air pushes around you, fills
with birds, yellow wings and eyes.

III

Bow strung, he leaps from the balcony
to the floor below, watching the dancers
drift like small beasts in summer, turning
quietly between the columns, slowly
over the stone floor. No one looks up.
He fits an arrow to his string, circles
behind the great chairs. Each dancer comes
across his eye. He singles one off,
near the orchestra, near one of the marble
pillars reflecting the autumnal colors
of the room, the lights from the chandelier.
Crouching, he moves closer. She turns gently
to her music, releasing the scent that attracts him.
He stops within the shadow, draws back the string,
and sighting over her left breast, shoots.
She falls. No sound is made. He runs to her,
lifts her and, still running, moves toward
the stair, disappears into the darkness above.

IV

Lifting itself, a column of marble, veined
and pink, a woman's arm, rising to a lack of stars.
They move between the columns,
over thick carpets, so many hills,
valleys to sink into. This is his place.
She turns to him; the reception desk
tapers into the darkness of other rooms,
not hers. He can touch the columns,
let his hand move into them and up
to a ceiling he has heard about.
They climb into big chairs, sleep
on the cushions. Somewhere bells
are always ringing.

Waking, she is gone and he goes after her,
through passages without doors. At times
the ceiling drops quickly, grazes his head,
at times the rug rises to it. He opens doors
with walls behind them. He meets important people
who talk of errands he forgets.
He meets an old man on a tall stool, looks up
to his feet; the man's words break like smoke
around him, speaking of something he should do.
The man's voice is a bell. Stewards pass
carrying plates with metal covers.

V

THE GUEST

I have always been lucky. When I first
came I was given the best rooms. There is
always the smell of apples. The linen is fresh.
Already the cooks know my ways, and at dinner
what I want is there when I come. I
don't have to ask. There is a woman
in the room next to mine who always
smiles when we meet. I spoke to her
at dinner. Her skin is as clear as glass.
At times I can almost see the bones,
white feathers stretching along her arms.
She promised to meet me and everything
went well. Always I have prided myself
on having a certain knack. We met
in the green room. I touched her face,
her arms. The room was filled with birds.
Their wings whipped our faces like small gloves.

VI

Running now, he turns from place to place,
his feet make no sound on the carpets. Each room
is empty. The walls bend, covered with pictures
he can almost touch. Landscapes, forests ending
in a growth of churches, towns. There are no
boats on the rivers, mountains push the stars
with white fingers. The pictures are bending
towards him. There is a man tied to a post,
others stand back, shoot him with arrows.
Faster, his feet barely touch the red floor.
All corners fall to him. A man on a plunging
white horse, sand in all directions.
A girl on a high swing at the moment
of rest before falling back. Her arm
extends from the rope, her fingers reaching
precariously out of the canvas, the gilt frame.
All rooms are empty.

She drops through a shaft of mirrors; the walls
reflect the image of her quick descent.
She hears nothing, is not afraid. Corridors
open from the mirrors, long halls of ropes
to catch a new way, leading to attics, dark
blue rooms with flowered arches, marble floors
so clear that each foot falls upon itself.
She sees her body all around her, arms
and legs extended. She watches the patterns
of her face, falls through the darkness
of her eyes. There are too many doors
for directions. She may stop when she wishes.

VII

I have not been here before. All night
I was kept awake by the sound of bells.
No one would tell me about them. Rising
in the morning, I found that the shutters
would not open. A maid filled the basin
with hot water. A blue basin with a thin
crack on one side. I spoke of it.
Her teeth are like small red stones.
At night the canopy over my bed
sways as if in a wind. I told her about
the shutters. Her promises are like silk.
I sell dresses. There are many things
she would like. At breakfast, I
was the only one, blue china,
a pot of coffee to myself. The linen
was so white I could see my face,
staring up, watching me as I ate.
All day I have been walking,
looking for my room. The bed
has a canopy and at night the covers
sway as if in a wind.

VIII

THE PREY

All day she has managed to stay
a few rooms ahead of him. Sometimes
she sees him, can feel his eyes move
through her, searching her body, looking
for what will ease his hunger. She runs.
Sometimes he is armed, his knife catches
the light, hurls it toward her. She can
barely get away. She can feel his hands
on her skin, scraping, moving in
to her flesh, tearing away the skin.
She runs, twisting through the people;
breaking across the carpets into valleys.
Even when she sleeps she can hear
his feet brushing the floor behind her.
They are like bells. Not all the rooms
have doors. Hundreds of ropes connect them.

IX

He is on the north side where the wind
is forever in the rooms. The furniture keeps
changing its shape. The rug clutches his feet with
tiny hands. He can't see across the room. The wind
pulls at his clothing, his face, but cannot
change him. Small animals fill the air. People flow
out of themselves, flutter like strips of cloth. He
shelters by the wall, avoiding the weight of the air.
He can't stay here, must go on, his feet
pull him backwards, away from the doors.
His fingers tear into the wall. Small birds
fill the air. They look like her. There are
too many faces for all the people.

She is as quiet as her room. Her chair
fits tightly around her. Somewhere inside
she is attempting to claw her way out. Her mind
is filled with ropes. Doors float down
a yellow river. She is the river and must
not touch the bank, must not touch
the edges of her skin. The water begins
to move faster, away from the banks, the doors
start to spin, are pulled down out of sight.
The river is red. Everything she touches drowns.
She has become her chair, floats in the softness
of her cushions. The water rises above her head.

X

THE ROOM

The people crowd together in the center
of the room, like arrows standing together,
like pieces of cloth sewn together,
like nothing. Each moves slightly
but attracts no attention. Men in black
circle around them, carrying out their wishes.
The faces shift into each other, become
each other, flow down onto the floor,
into a large pool covered with flowers,
roses, lilies. The men in black tend
the flowers, quietly prune the leaves
and dead buds, bring fresh water. The flowers
turn in on themselves, release black petals
that float to the surface, are taken by the men.
The perfume pushes against the walls
in great waves. The walls fall back.
Children come to gather the flowers.

XI

THE CARETAKER

If something breaks, they tell me
and I fix it. Like clocks, my tools
refinish or repair all that is given me.
I ask no questions. Once they came
and led me to a green room in the cellar.
Parts of the machine covered the floor.
They didn't move. It wasn't difficult.
My place is behind the running stair.
A small bell calls me when I'm needed,
but I don't have to go. Last week
one of the rooms began to turn in on itself,
it's like watching the petals of a flower,
or a spider dying. I was too busy.
I have my own life. All around me
there are things to occupy my time.
Children plague me with questions.

XII

She is in the center of the blue room
surrounded by flowers. The marble floor
carries off her reflection. Somewhere
she can hear herself talking. Her words fall
like small faces into the flowers, the brilliance
of the floor. He finds her there, moves
towards her, forcing his feet one after
the other towards her. Bells fall
around him. He reaches her, touches
her cheek. Her words break over him like water.
He moves into her, his hands move into her body.
He is her body, turning around him, colors
turning together. His mouth is filled
with her words. Their body flows down
through itself, into the floor. There is
no noise that will wake them. Together
they are one high sound.

Part Five

Name–Burning

Ashes, the dissonance of unicorns: the edges
of my written name begin to curl, the ink
still visible through the fire. In absence of stars,
my natality card remains safely in Washington.
The sleep of animal counterparts: like frogs,
the consonants hold their sounds long after
the vowels have died. Poor vowels, asleep
in their boxes, dreaming of proclamations
and Latin verbs. The man at the top of the stairs
offers his assistance, keeping the silence of mice
orchestrating the works of Satie, the music
of children alone in rooms. He will gather
the seeds of new sounds, fit letters together,
making a puzzle of the United States. Vermont
lying buried in the deep South; all in his head.
A disbelief in unicorns and concurring beasts,
he fills their places, planting his sounds,
waters them, watches them grow, their blossoms
beginning to break forth jointly. The ink is gone.
Washington has wandered off the map. Somewhere
in Montana, a bear, waking, hears his name,
shakes himself, grumbles off through fields
of flowering clover.

Of Stones

There are easier things than sorting the stones.
From each I expect one gift, redemptive,
defining the silence; each is a fist
to be cracked open. Begin with the first:
here is a place for my head,
suddenly heavy; and there is my old name
in granite, a delicate italic. Discard it.
We have used it too many times.
From another which has traveled far
beneath the ocean, a long story, its secrets
and knowledge of fish, persistent in being
no more than they seem. Crack it open.
A third to aim: victims stretch from my
fingers like banners welcoming me home;
I have shuffled their faces through too many mirrors.
And others from the mountains, rain and rock-ground;
the beginnings and ends of stones; bones;
sand, useful to walk in, bury in;
the movement of treadmills; turning, walking,
and remaining sand: the loss of beginnings.
The scattered stones of conscience, thrown stones,
falling stones—slim consolation.

A dog bears grudges and forgiveness
equally. I lack the skill
and persist in burial, a place to be mined.
Tell me a long story about fish and
let there be music in it: The Carrier
of Big Stones. Let me find changes,
find the texture of my fingers, hands,
becoming the texture of stone. Crack it.
The stones will grow soft through proximity.

A new sufficiency: the ability to step back
and hurl stones gracefully at trees
and red birds. But where's the beauty of it?
The beauty of the word become stone;
and again, the word as stone. Build
a wall of it, make a cake of it. Open
your mouth. Eat it. Then let it return,
becoming the action and passion of category:
the movement, division, the family and falling into,
the sum of the answers, the comfort of stones.

Passing the Word

The poem as object; communicable; naked
as a mannikin after closing, stripped
between dressings, wig torn off, arms and legs
piled on the floor—the ability to rebuild,
a movement from nothing. The poem as bell
and the mannikin's head as clapper: a silent bell,
insistently proclaiming. Dogs stir. A cat
moves into shadow: now a jungle, now a tiger.
The poem at your front door at three in the morning,
leaning on a bell echoing in both of you,
which becomes both of you, coming together
from different directions. And caught by the sound,
you stumble downstairs; a single slipper and slap
of a bare foot; tugging at your robe; finding
the light which doesn't work. You open the door
and there is the mannikin dressed in dark silks—
a jumble of arms and legs for you to assemble;
its face white except for the mouth, a red river
between the ears; and the eyes which are empty.
And you would say something, searching for anger
beneath stones, some counter-blow, some final
definition. But you wait too long and now your face,
at best never more than tacked on, begins to slide,
drip like a bad tap between your slipper
and one bare foot. And you would move your arms,
legs, but suddenly they are moving into you,
into your body like sleeves turned inside out.
You are unnecessarily afraid. There's no harm here.
You can refuse to accept it and in the morning

it will be gone and you will have forgotten it,
rearranged your face with a nail in the forehead.
You will leave your front steps as it will have left
the bed you have opened to it and your wife with
her half smile and dreams of trees heavy with apples.

When You're Dancing, Make the Whole World Dance With You

Bring my name upon a platter. I have danced
long enough. My audience applauds. I applaud.
My hands sound like hundreds. There are no
answers in that language. I have seen no
burning bush. I would turn away no golden calf
that showed an interest. I have named all the names
forwards and backwards and the sky does not darken.
I am like a lot of Jacobs wrestling together—
our clothes torn into thin strips, feather-like.
There were angels here, but left without speaking.
On a farther shore the usual old man with the usual
one eye and slouch hat beckons to someone taller,
darker and more strange. Stones will not attract him.

Doors shut. Closets are behind them, trunks laced
with red silk. Together we will fill them. Already
I know your ways. I have walked down city streets.
I have followed you into shops, watched you make
your small but necessary purchases and followed
when you left. I know the sidewalks to your home.
I am right behind you. I will whisper in your ear
in a dark moment. I will strip your name from you
like an Indian after a scalp. I will find all your names.
Flutes will stop. Drums will be broken. The only
dance left is the last one. Who shall lead us
up the hill, swaying in single file? There's a door
at the top. That knocking has always been within us.

Finding the Direction

It is quiet. It is a place where
the grass sleeps and I have come to it.
When it wakes, my clocks will turn twice
and discover the necessity of stopping.
Buses pass such places. Their passengers
are mostly asleep. One light in the back
and a man who has read that mystery before.
Who calls to the deaf? To cross water,
to learn the knowledge of fire, I shall
move myself backwards. A crab has always
forgotten something and dies in pursuit.
Awake and moving, I know of houses where
my pockets have emptied themselves of essentials.
Backwards, I shall find them. There is
too much shouting in a forward direction.
There is no analogy in sleep. The man
reading does not experience the road,
has forgotten his family. To discover
the fence posts, then to reach the gate.
Awakened, the grass shifts, twisting
within itself, as I do, scurrying. The teeth
of some dragons are very small. Plant them
carefully. Water and watch the ground.

New Approaches

Now I shall begin to steal. Come to me,
lovely, with wide open arms.
At the rag ends of fields my words
are crouching. They know of a freight
better than the one they've been riding.
It is seen in the distance. It is here.
It's gone. A grey man waves from the caboose.
I know that red flag, have seen it mocking
from attics and high places. There are no stairs.
There are weights too heavy to be shifted easily.
Let me check your rings for stones. Where are
those arms? They send postcards from Italy
showing Venetian piazzas littered with pigeons.
They are in the background, ringless, with cameras
at ready. They do not know the sun.
There are voices in Tulsa which would recognize
mine. I have searched their pockets and found
old coins, cats' feet, and numerous glass objects
which will never be pearls. I am surrounded
by temporary pleasures. There is no gain in profit.
A stone is my object. I must imitate its contours
and stolid expression. If I catch you looking at the sun
I'll take it. For a short time you will see nothing
and lose all names. While I, in a dark place,
have a new world before me.

The Ways of Keys

The justice of bells, persistent in ringing.
A dark lantern emitting a single ray, one
red beam, sending it forth. Just
as the sun, dropping behind fences,
sends out its last light to fields
quiet with horses. There are too many things,
too much to touch upon. I have become an absence
and my name slides from the vacancies.
I have left my tongue and small list
of essential words in a locker at a station
surrounded by the old and poor
staring into their hands. If you speak,
I can only show you the key which is soundless,
point to the number which is empty.
There are no words. They slip from my fingers.
I see their fragments far beneath me,
flickering like candles about to go out.
I would learn to lie, speak only by number;
set wings upon the key and a small voice
to tell stories; to fly over the land, wrapped
in its mutterings, babble justice in the ears
of Mount Rushmore. Or I would keep a train,
small and electric; stock the cars with words,
fragments stolen from churches, schools;
learn the sly ways into your houses at night;
sing into sleeping ears of caves and rivers,
the death of trees, the silence of their dying,

the silence of the word as word.
There are too many things.
Repeat it to me: the justice of bells.
Then give me the sound and let it be
circular, going round with no knowledge of stopping.
Let a dark lantern be placed in the circle
and let me lie down by it, becoming
both entrance and exit of light. Let me
be the door and the lock. Let me
learn the ways of keys.

Stephen Dobyns

Stephen Dobyns was born in East Orange, New
Jersey in 1941; he was raised in New Jersey,
Michigan, Virginia, Pennsylvania and Michigan
again, moving every year or two. He was educated at
Shimer College, Wayne State University and
The University of Iowa. He spent two years in
college news service work, two years as a college
instructor and 19 months as a reporter for the
Detroit News.